braintrails.org

Copyright © 2020 by Braintrails.org

Braintrails.org
Minneapolis, MN

www.braintrails.org
Written and illustrated by Nick Lowe

All rights reserved. This book or any portion thereof may not be reproduced or used in any manner whatsoever without the express written permission of the publisher except for the use of brief quotations in a book review.
First Printing, 2020

Printed in the United States of America

ISBN 978-1-7355006-2-1

Alpha-Animals

Have fun finding letters in animals, learning letter sounds, and drawing these animals.

Sit down and turn the pages with your little one. Engage them with questions like: What are the bugs doing and where is the caterpillar? What animal do you see? Is it the Mom, Dad, or baby? Letters make sounds and words; what letter is in this animal and what is its sound?

Older kids can have fun drawing these cute little animals, writing their names in animals, and making their own.

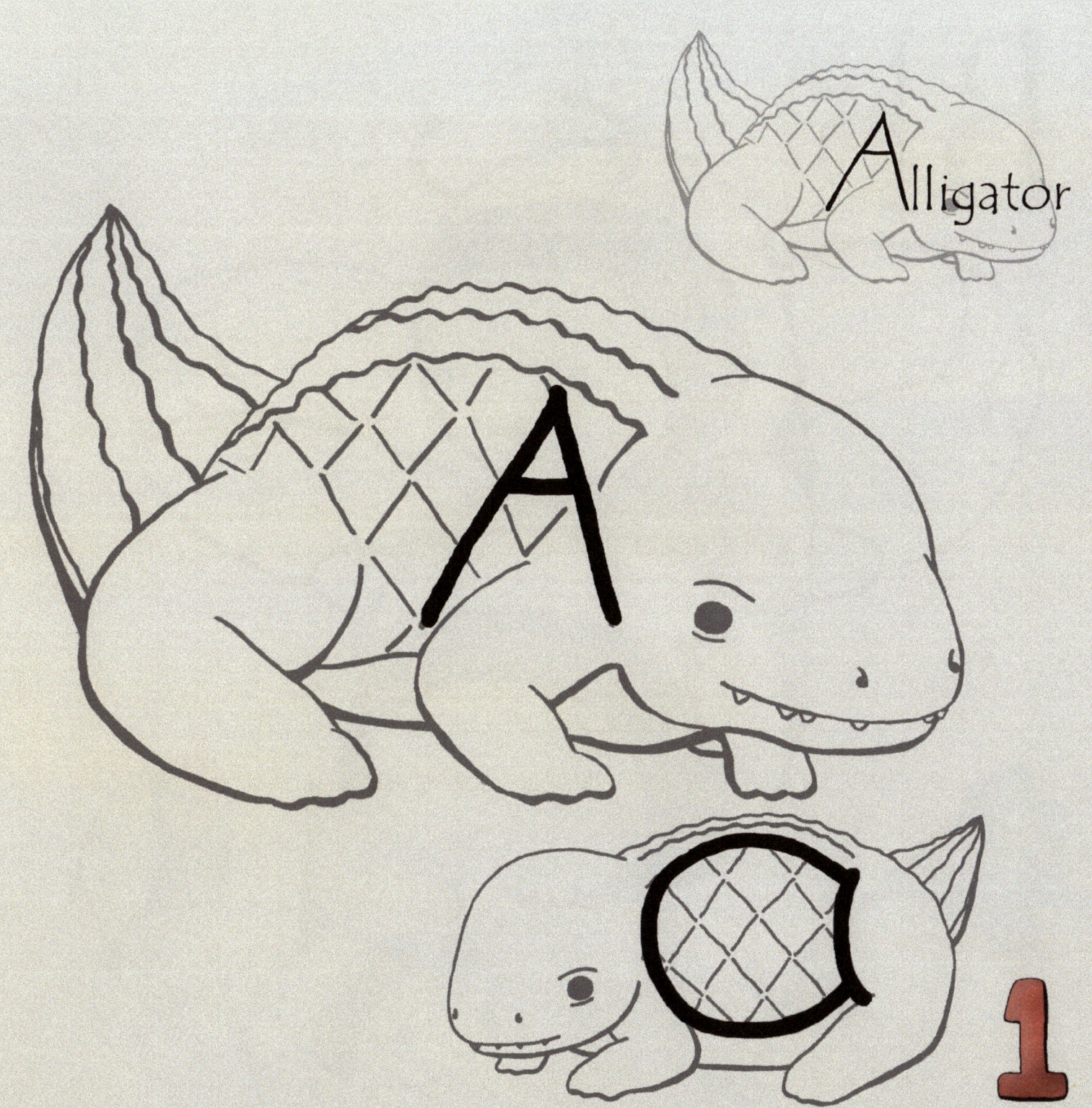

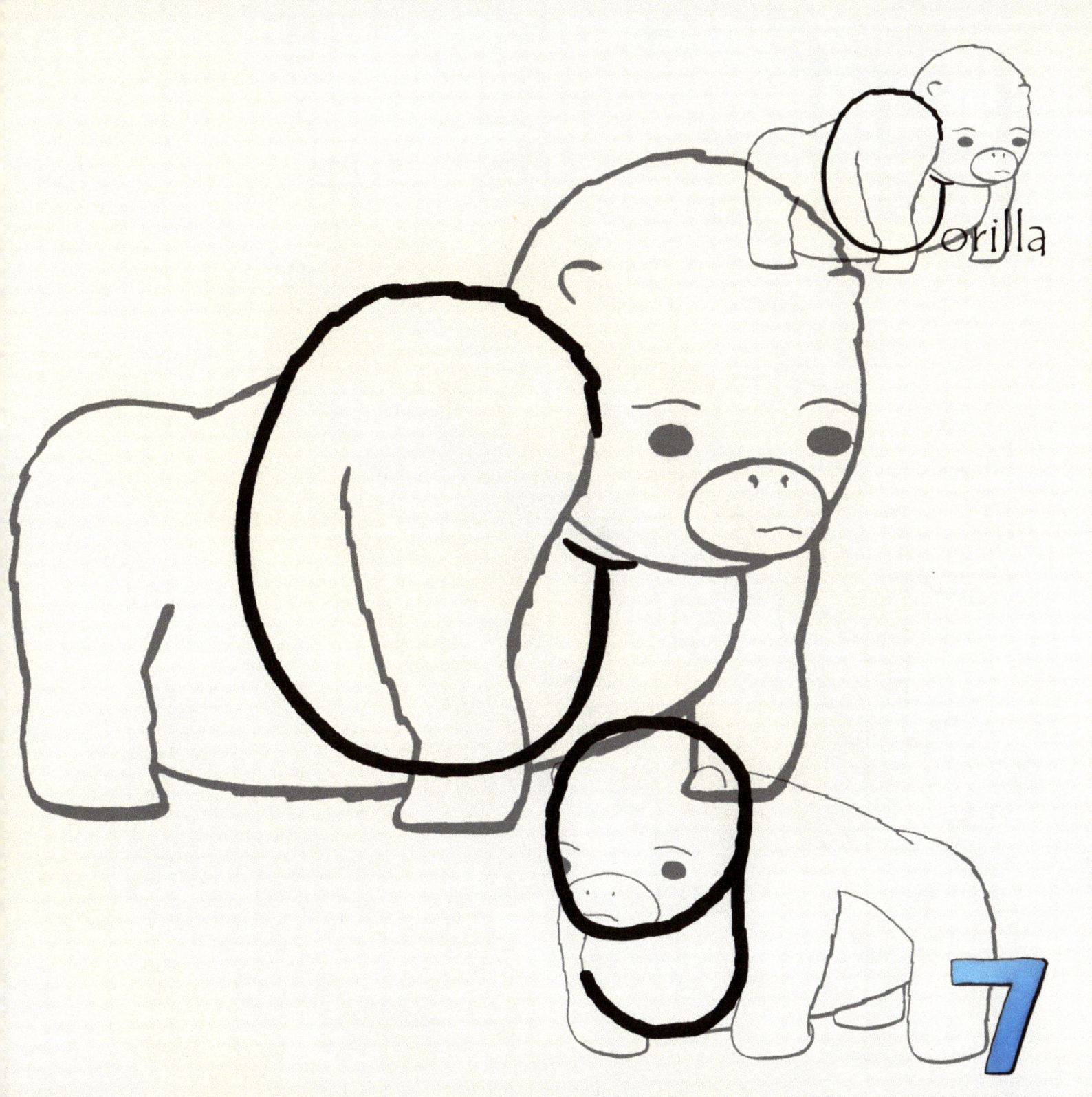

Gorilla

7

Ii

Kk

Mm

Penguin

16

Qq

Quail

17

Rr

Snake

Make your mouth like these kids to make the letter sounds!

Keep a look out for our next book at:
braintrails.org

The Alpha-Animals ebook contains interactive content including letter sounds and videos, as well as printable coloring pages.
To receive the Alpha-Animals ebook for free go to braintrails.org and enter the code "connect" at checkout.

Sign up for our newsletter to receive information on early learning and new braintrails.

CPSIA information can be obtained
at www.ICGtesting.com
Printed in the USA
BVHW022046281120
594422BV00009B/85